To

_____

From

_____

A Woman's
Treasury
of
GRACE

The quoted ideas expressed in this book (but not scripture verses) are not, in all cases, exact quotations, as some have been edited for clarity and brevity. In all cases, the author has attempted to maintain the speaker's original intent. In some cases, quoted material for this book was obtained from secondary sources, primarily print media. While every effort was made to ensure the accuracy of these sources, the accuracy cannot be guaranteed. For additions, deletions, corrections or clarifications in future editions of this text, please write FAMILY CHRISTIAN PRESS.

Scripture quotations are taken from:

The Holy Bible, King James Version

The Holy Bible, New International Version (NIV) Copyright © 1973, 1978, 1984, by International Bible Society. Used by permission of Zondervan Publishing House. All rights reserved.

The Holy Bible, New King James Version (NKJV) Copyright © 1982 by Thomas Nelson, Inc. Used by permission.

The New American Standard Bible®, (NASB) Copyright © 1960, 1962, 1963, 1968, 1971, 1972, 1973, 1975, 1977, 1995 by The Lockman Foundation. Used by permission.

Holy Bible, New Living Translation, (NLT) Copyright © 1996. Used by permission of Tyndale House Publishers, Inc., Wheaton, Illinois 60189. All rights reserved.

New Century Version®. (NCV) Copyright © 1987, 1988, 1991 by Word Publishing, a division of Thomas Nelson, Inc. All rights reserved. Used by permission.

The Message (MSG)- This edition issued by contractual arrangement with NavPress, a division of The Navigators, U.S.A. Originally published by NavPress in English as THE MESSAGE: The Bible in Contemporary Language copyright 2002-2003 by Eugene Peterson. All rights reserved.

The Holman Christian Standard Bible™ (HCSB) Copyright © 1999, 2000, 2001 by Holman Bible Publishers. Used by permission.

Cover Design by Kim Russell / Wahoo Designs
Page Layout by Bart Dawson

ISBN 1-58334-233-8

Printed in the United States of America

FAMILY
CHRISTIAN
PRESS

Table of Contents

Introduction

*J*esus is the spiritual sun that gives warmth, light, and life to the world. Christ died on the cross so that we might have eternal life. This gift, freely given from God's only Son, is the priceless possession of everyone who accepts Him as Lord and Savior.

Thankfully, God's grace is not an earthly reward for righteous behavior; it is, instead, a blessed spiritual gift. When we welcome Christ into our hearts, we are saved by His grace. The familiar words from the book of Ephesians make God's promise perfectly clear: "For it is by grace you have been saved, through faith—and this not from yourselves, it is the gift of God—not by works, so that no one can boast" (2:8-9 NIV).

As a Christian woman living in these troubled times, you may be easily sidetracked by the distractions and demands of everyday living. This treasury of quotations and Bible verses is intended to remind you of the priceless gift of God's grace. May you experience His grace—and may you share His Good News—with a world that desperately needs both.

Grace and God's Will

After this manner therefore
pray ye…. Thy kingdom come.
Thy will be done in earth,
as it is in heaven.

Matthew 6:9-10 KJV

God created you for a purpose—within that purpose, you will find God's grace, God's presence, God's love, and God's abundance.

Whether you realize it or not, God has a plan for your life, a divine calling, a direction in which He is leading you. When you accept God's gift of grace and establish a genuine relationship with Him, He will begin, in time, to make His purposes known.

Sometimes, God's intentions will be clear to you; other times, God's plan for you may seem uncertain at best. But even on those difficult days when you are unsure which way to turn, you must never lose sight of these overriding facts: God created you for a reason; He has given you a particular set of tools; He has important work for you to do; and He's waiting patiently for you to do it. The next step is up to you.

In the center of a hurricane there
is absolute quiet and peace.
There is no safer place
than in the center of
the will of God.

Corrie ten Boom

God has a present will for your life.
It is neither chaotic nor utterly exhausting.
In the midst of many good choices vying
for your time, He will give you the discernment
to recognize what is best.

Beth Moore

What of the great prayer Jesus taught us to pray?
It is for His kingdom and His will,
yet we ought not to ask it
unless we ourselves are prepared to cooperate.

Elisabeth Elliot

There is only one way to love God:
to take not a single step without him, and
to follow with a brave heart wherever he leads.

Fénelon

You will show me the path of life;
in Your presence is fullness of joy;
at Your right hand are pleasures forevermore.

Psalm 16:11 NKJV

The center of power is not to be found in
summit meetings or in peace conferences.
It is not in Peking or Washington or
the United Nations, but rather where a child of
God prays in the power of the Spirit for
God's will to be done in her life, in her home,
and in the world around her.

Ruth Bell Graham

O, that I could consecrate myself, soul and body,
to his service forever; O, that I could give myself
up to him, so as never more to attempt to be
my own or to have any will or affection
improper for those conformed to him.

Lottie Moon (missionary to China)

God is working in you to help you want to do
and be able to do what pleases him.

Philippians 2:13 NCV

Walk in the daylight of
God's will because then
you will be safe;
you will not stumble.

❧

Anne Graham Lotz

But what happens when we live God's way?
He brings gifts into our lives, much the same
way that fruit appears in an orchard, things like
affection for others, exuberance about life, serenity.
We develop a willingness to stick with things,
a sense of compassion in the heart, and
a conviction that a basic holiness permeates
things and people. We find ourselves involved
in loyal commitments, not needing to force
our way in life, able to marshal and
direct our energies wisely.

Galatians 5:22-23 MSG

How often it occurs to me, as it must to you,
that is far easier simply to cooperate with God!

Beth Moore

Teach me Your way, O LORD;
I will walk in Your truth.

Psalm 86:11 NKJV

I believe that in every time and place it is within
our power to acquiesce in the will of God—
and what peace it brings to do so!

Elisabeth Elliot

Surrender to the Lord is not a tremendous sacrifice,
not an agonizing performance.
It is the most sensible thing you can do.

Corrie ten Boom

And the peace of God, which surpasses
every thought, will guard your hearts and your
minds in Christ Jesus. Finally brothers, whatever
is true, whatever is honorable, whatever is just,
whatever is pure, whatever is lovely, whatever is
commendable—if there is any moral excellence
and if there is any praise—dwell on these things.

Philippians 4:7-8 HCSB

Grace and God's Plan

"For I know the plans I have for you,"
declares the LORD, "plans to prosper you
and not to harm you, plans to give you
hope and a future. Then you will call
upon me and come and pray to me,
and I will listen to you."

Jeremiah 29:11-12 NIV

God has things He wants you to do and places He wants you to go. The most important decision of your life is, of course, your commitment to accept Jesus Christ as your personal Lord and Savior. And, once your eternal destiny is secured, you will undoubtedly ask yourself the question "What now, Lord?" If you earnestly seek God's will for your life, you will find it . . . in time.

As you seek to discover God's path for your life, you should study His Holy Word and be ever watchful for His signs. You should associate with fellow Christians who will encourage your spiritual growth, and you should listen to that inner voice that speaks to you in the quiet moments of your daily devotionals.

Rest assured: God is here, and He intends to use you in wonderful, unexpected ways. He desires to lead you along a path of His choosing. Your challenge is to watch, to listen . . . and to follow.

With God, it's never
"Plan B" or "second best."
It's always "Plan A."
And, if we let Him,
He'll make something beautiful
of our lives.

Gloria Gaither

Ours is an intentional God, brimming over with motive and mission. He never does things capriciously or decides with the flip of a coin.

Joni Eareckson Tada

The secret you stumble on is this: If, once hurt, you open your heart and let God take you by the hand, he will lead you to a better place than you have known.

Paula Rinehart

There is something incredibly comforting about knowing that the Creator is in control of your life.

Lisa Whelchel

For whoever does the will of God is My brother and My sister and mother.

Mark 3:35 NKJV

In God's economy, whether He is making a flower
or a human soul, nothing ever comes to nothing.
The losses are His way of accomplishing the gains.

Elisabeth Elliot

God will never lead you where His strength
cannot keep you.

Barbara Johnson

Mark it down: things do not "just happen."
There is a God-arranged plan for this world of ours,
which includes a specific plan for you.

Charles Swindoll

The only Person who has ever brought
sustained power and purpose into my life is
the living person of God. The only words
that keep making sense are His words.
The only way that always stands is His way.

Angela Thomas

And we know that in all things
God works for the good
of those who love him,
who have been called
according to his purpose.

Romans 8:28 NIV

O Lord, thank You that Your side of the embroidery
of our life is always perfect. That is such a comfort
when our side is sometimes so mixed up.

Corrie ten Boom

What God has started in all of us
He has promised to finish.

Gloria Gaither

Surely goodness and mercy shall follow me all
the days of my life: and I will dwell in
the house of the LORD for ever.

Psalm 23:6 KJV

There has never been the slightest doubt in
my mind that the God who started this great work
in you would keep at it and bring it to a flourishing
finish on the very day Christ Jesus appears.

Philippians 1:6 MSG

And do not be conformed to this world, but
be transformed by the renewing of your mind,
that you may prove what is that good and
acceptable and perfect will of God.

Romans 12:2 NKJV

God wants us to serve Him with a willing spirit,
one that would choose no other way.

Beth Moore

I'm convinced that there is nothing that can
happen to me in this life that is not precisely
designed by a sovereign Lord to give me
the opportunity to learn to know Him.

Elisabeth Elliot

Trust the LORD your God with all your heart
and lean not on your own understanding;
in all your ways acknowledge him,
and he will make your paths straight.

Proverbs 3:5-6 NIV

Grace and God's Comfort

Even though I walk through
the valley of the shadow of death,
I will fear no evil,
for you are with me;
your rod and your staff,
they comfort me.

Psalm 23:4 NIV

Even the most faithful Christian woman may find her courage tested by the inevitable disappointments and tragedies of life. After all, we live in a world filled with uncertainty, hardship, sickness, and danger. Old Man Trouble, it seems, is never too far from the front door.

When we focus upon our fears and our doubts, we may find many reasons to lie awake at night and fret about the uncertainties of the coming day. A better strategy, of course, is to focus not upon our fears but, instead, upon our God.

God is as near as your next heartbeat, and He is in control. He offers salvation to all His children, including you. God is your shield and your strength; you are His forever. So don't focus your thoughts upon the fears of the day. Instead, trust God's plan and His eternal love for you. And remember: whatever the size of your challenge, God is bigger.

Put your hand into
the hand of God.
He gives the calmness
and serenity of heart and soul.

Mrs. Charles E. Cowman

When God allows extraordinary trials for
His people, He prepares extraordinary
comforts for them.

Corrie ten Boom

We all go through pain and sorrow,
but the presence of God, like a warm, comforting
blanket, can shield us and protect us, and
allow the deep inner joy to surface,
even in the most devastating circumstances.

Barbara Johnson

Pour out your heart to God and tell Him how
you feel. Be real, be honest, and when you
get it all out, you'll start to feel the gradual covering
of God's comforting presence.

Bill Hybels

There is a place of quiet rest, there is a place of
comfort sweet, near to the heart of God.

Cleland B. McAfee

Praise be to the God and
Father of our Lord Jesus Christ. God is
the Father who is full
of mercy and all comfort.
He comforts us every time
we have trouble, so when others have
trouble, we can comfort them with the
same comfort
God gives us.

2 Corinthians 1:3–4 NCV

So often we think that to be encouragers we have
to produce great words of wisdom when, in fact,
a few simple syllables of sympathy and an arm
around the shoulder can often provide
much needed comfort.

Florence Littauer

Here is a simple, rule-of-thumb for behavior:
Ask yourself what you want people to do for you,
then grab the initiative and do it for them. Add up
God's Law and Prophets and this is what you get.

Matthew 7:12 MSG

When we Christians are too busy to care for each
other, we're simply too busy for our own good . . .
and for God's.

Marie T. Freeman

Kind words are like honey—sweet to the soul
and healthy for the body.

Proverbs 16:24 NLT

Jesus draws near to those who are afflicted
and persecuted and criticized and ostracized.

Anne Graham Lotz

We don't mend each other's brokenness;
we admit our needs and let that draw us
to each other and to God.

Paula Rinehart

I never look at the masses as my responsibility.
I look at the individual. I can love only one person
at a time. I can feed only one person at a time.
Just one, one, one. You get closer to Christ
by coming closer to each other.

Mother Teresa

Verily I say unto you, Inasmuch as ye have done it
unto one of the least of these my brethren,
ye have done it unto me.

Matthew 25:40 KJV

He treats us as sons, and all he asks in return
is that we shall treat Him as a Father
whom we can trust without anxiety.
We must take the son's place of dependence
and trust, and we must let Him keep
the father's place of care and responsibility.

Hannah Whitall Smith

Snuggle in God's arms.
When you are hurting, when you feel lonely or
left out, let Him cradle you, comfort you,
reassure you of His all-sufficient power and love.

Kay Arthur

Be anxious for nothing, but in everything by prayer
and supplication, with thanksgiving,
let your requests be made known to God.

Philippians 4:6 NKJV

Cast all your anxiety on him because
he cares for you.

1 Peter 5:7 NIV

When you pass through the waters,
I will be with you; and through the rivers,
they shall not overflow you. When you walk
through the fire, you shall not be burned,
nor shall the flame scorch you.
For I am the LORD your God,
The Holy One of Israel, your Savior.

Isaiah 43:2-3 NKJV

If I am walking along the street with
a very disfiguring hole in the back of my dress,
of which I am in ignorance, it is certainly
a very great comfort to me to have a kind friend
who will tell me of it. And similarly, it is indeed
a comfort to know that there is always abiding
with me a divine, all-seeing Comforter,
who will reprove me for all my faults
and will not let me go on in
a fatal unconsciousness of them.

Hannah Whitall Smith

One of the things I've learned in my walk through
the Bible is to seek not healing, but the Healer;
not love, but the Lover; not gifts, but the Giver;
not answers, but the One who knows all
the answers. The God of all comfort
will comfort us even when
there are no explanations.

Susan Wales

The more comfortable we are with mystery
in our journey, the more rest
we will know along the way.

John Eldredge

In the worst temptations nothing can help us
but faith that God's Son has put on flesh,
sits at the right hand of the Father, and prays for us.
There is no mightier comfort.

Martin Luther

On the darkest day of your life,
God is still in charge. Take comfort in that.

Marie T. Freeman

Oh! what a Savior,
gracious to all,
Oh! how His blessings
round us fall,
Gently to comfort,
kindly to cheer,
Sleeping or waking,
God is near.

Fanny Crosby

Grace and
God's Protection

God is my shield,
saving those whose hearts
are true and right.

Psalm 7:10 NLT

In a world filled with dangers and temptations, God is the ultimate armor. In a world filled with misleading messages, God's Word is the ultimate truth. In a world filled with more frustrations than we can count, God's Son offers the ultimate peace. Will you accept God's peace and wear God's armor against the dangers of our world?

Sometimes, in the crush of everyday life, God may seem far away, but He is not. God is everywhere you have ever been and everywhere you will ever go. He is with you night and day; He knows your thoughts and your prayers. His is your ultimate Protector. And, when you earnestly seek His protection, you will find it because He is here—always—waiting patiently for you to reach out to Him.

Prayer is our pathway
not only to divine protection
but also to a personal,
intimate relationship with God.

Shirley Dobson

He is within and without.
His Spirit dwells within me. His armor protects me.
He goes before me and is behind me.

Mary Morrison Suggs

When you are in the furnace,
your Father keeps His eye on the clock
and His hand on the thermostat.
He knows just how much we can take.

Warren Wiersbe

And God, in his mighty power,
will protect you until you receive this salvation,
because you are trusting him.

1 Peter 1:5 NLT

He goes before us, follows behind us,
and hems us safe inside the realm of His protection.

Beth Moore

We can take great comfort that God never sleeps—
so we can.

Dianna Booher

In all the old castles of England, there was a place
called the keep. It was always the strongest
and best protected place in the castle,
and in it were hidden all who were weak
and helpless and unable to defend themselves
in times of danger. Shall we be afraid to hide
ourselves in the keeping power of our Divine
Keeper, who neither slumbers nor sleeps,
and who has promised to preserve our going out
and our coming in, from this time forth
and even forever more?

Hannah Whitall Smith

Then King Nebuchadnezzar was so surprised that he jumped to his feet. He asked the men who advised him, "Didn't we tie up only three men and throw them into the fire?" They answered, "Yes, O king." The king said, "Look! I see four men walking around in the fire. They are not tied up, and they are not burned. The fourth man looks like a son of the gods."

Daniel 3:24-25 NCV

As sure as God puts his children in the furnace, he will be in the furnace with them.

C. H. Spurgeon

The LORD keeps watch over you as you come and go, both now and forever.

Psalm 121:8 NLT

It is faith that what happens to me matters to God as well as to me that gives me joy, that promises me that I am eternally the subject of God's compassion, and that assures me that the compassion was manifested most brilliantly when God came to us in a stable in Bethlehem.

Madeleine L'Engle

There is not only fear, but terrible danger, for the life unguarded by God.

Oswald Chambers

It is an act of the will to allow God to be our refuge. Otherwise we live outside of his love and protection, wondering why we feel alone and afraid.

Mary Morrison Suggs

In the multitude of my anxieties within me, Your comforts delight my soul.

Psalm 94:19 NKJV

A mighty fortress is our God,
a bulwark never failing
Our helper He, amid the flood
of mortal ills prevailing
For still our ancient foe doth
seek to work us woe
His craft and power are great,
And, armed with cruel hate,
On earth is not his equal.

Martin Luther

Gather the riches of God's promises which
can strengthen you in the time when
there will be no freedom.

Corrie ten Boom

Our future may look fearfully intimidating,
yet we can look up to the Engineer of the Universe,
confident that nothing escapes His attention or
slips out of the control of those strong hands.

Elisabeth Elliot

God has promised us abundance, peace,
and eternal life. These treasures are ours for
the asking; all we must do is claim them.
One of the great mysteries of life is why on earth
so many of us wait so very long to claim them.

Marie T. Freeman

Only believe, don't fear. Our Master, Jesus, always
watches over us, and no matter what
the persecution, Jesus will surely overcome it.

Lottie Moon (missionary to China)

I am grateful that when even a single sparrow
falls to the ground, God knows—and understands.

Ruth Bell Graham

A God wise enough to create me and the world
I live in is wise enough to watch out for me.

Philip Yancey

For the eyes of the Lord are on the righteous
and his ears are attentive to their prayer,
but the Lord is against those who do evil.

1 Peter 3:12 NIV

Grace and
God's Guidance

In all your ways
acknowledge Him,
and He shall direct your paths.

Proverbs 3:6 NKJV

*P*salm 37 teaches us that, "The steps of the godly are directed by the LORD. He delights in every detail of their lives" (v. 23 NLT). In other words, God is intensely interested in each of us, and He will guide our steps if we serve Him obediently.

When we sincerely offer heartfelt prayers to our Heavenly Father, He will give direction and meaning to our lives—but He won't force us to follow Him. To the contrary, God has given us the free will to seek His guidance and follow His commandments—or not.

Will you trust God to guide your steps? You should. When you entrust your life to Him completely and without reservation, God will give you the strength to meet any challenge, the courage to face any trial, and the wisdom to live in His righteousness and in His peace. Seek His guidance. When you do, your next step will be the right one.

*G*od will prove to you how good
and acceptable and perfect
His will is when He's got
His hands on the steering wheel
of your life.

Stuart & Jill Briscoe

Are you serious about wanting God's guidance to
become a personal reality in your life?
The first step is to tell God that you know
you can't manage your own life,
that you need his help.

Catherine Marshall

In all human affairs there are things both certain
and doubtful, and both are equally in the hands
of God, who is accustomed to guide to
a good end the causes that are just
and are sought with diligence.

Isabella of Spain

The Bible is not a guidebook to a theological
museum. It is a road map showing us the way
into neglected or even forgotten glories
of the living God.

Raymond Ortlund

God's guidance is even more important than common sense. I can declare that the deepest darkness is outshone by the light of Jesus.

Corrie ten Boom

If we want to hear God's voice, we must surrender our minds and hearts to Him.

Billy Graham

We have ample evidence that the Lord is able to guide. The promises cover every imaginable situation. All we need to do is to take the hand he stretches out.

Elisabeth Elliot

The LORD says, "I will make you wise and show you where to go. I will guide you and watch over you."

Psalm 32:8 NCV

God cannot lead the individual
who is not willing to give Him
a blank check with his life.

Catherine Marshall

Nothing happens by happenstance. I am not in the hands of fate, nor am I the victim of man's whims or the devil's ploys. There is One who sits above man, above Satan, and above all heavenly hosts as the ultimate authority of all the universe. That One is my God and my Father!

Kay Arthur

It's a bit like river rafting with an experienced guide. You may begin to panic when the guide steers you straight into a steep waterfall, especially if another course appears much safer. Yet, after you've emerged from the swirling depths and wiped the spray from your eyes, you see that just beyond the seemingly "safe" route was a series of jagged rocks. Your guide knew what he was doing after all.

Shirley Dobson

Reverence for the LORD is the foundation
of true wisdom. The rewards of wisdom
come to all who obey him.

Psalm 111:10 NLT

Only the LORD gives wisdom;
he gives knowledge and understanding.

Proverbs 2:6 NCV

If any of you lacks wisdom, he should ask God,
who gives generously to all without finding fault,
and it will be given to him.

James 1:5 NIV

Grace and God's Love

The unfailing love of
the LORD never ends!

Lamentations 3:22 NLT

*G*od's love for you is deeper and more profound than you can fathom. And now, precisely because you are a wondrous creation transformed by the grace of God, a question presents itself: What will you do in response to God's love? Will you ignore it or embrace it? Will you return it or neglect it? The decision, of course, is yours and yours alone.

When you embrace God's love, you are forever changed. When you embrace God's love, you feel differently about yourself, your neighbors, and your world. When you embrace God's love, you share His message and you obey His commandments.

When you accept the Father's grace and share His love, you are blessed here on earth and throughout all eternity. Accept His love today.

*J*esus loves us with fidelity, purity,
constancy, and passion,
no matter how imperfect we are.

Stormie Omartian

I think God knew that the message we sometimes
need to hear today is not what a great and
mighty God we serve but, rather, what a tender,
loving Father we have, even when He says no.

Lisa Whelchel

Love is not merely an attitude with which God
clothes Himself at certain times; rather, it is
an attribute that so permeates His being that
He could never divest Himself of it. To do so would
make Him less than God. Therefore,
whatever actions or commandments issue
forth from His throne must come from love.

Kay Arthur

Life with Christ is endless love;
without Him, it is a loveless end.

Billy Graham

There is no creature made who can realize
how much, how sweetly, and how tenderly
our Maker loves us. And therefore we can, with
His grace and His help, stand in spirit, gazing with
endless wonder at this lofty, immeasurable love—
beyond human scope—that the Almighty,
in His goodness, has for us.

Juliana of Norwich

In the wounds of the dying Savior,
see the love of the great I AM.

C. H. Spurgeon

Being loved by Him whose opinion matters most
gives us the security to risk loving, too—
even loving ourselves.

Gloria Gaither

Behold, behold
the wondrous love,
That ever flows from God above
Through Christ His only Son,
Who gave His precious blood
our souls to save.

Fanny Crosby

There is no pit so deep that God's love
is not deeper still.

Corrie ten Boom

The unfolding of our friendship with
the Father will be a never-ending revelation
stretching on into eternity.

Catherine Marshall

As we focus on His love and Word, in time
He will fill our void and loneliness,
and He will heal our pain.

Anita Corrine Donihue

I am convinced our hearts are not healthy
until they have been satisfied by
the only completely healthy love that exists:
the love of God Himself.

Beth Moore

We know how much
God loves us, and we have put
our trust in him. God is love,
and all who live in love live in God,
and God lives in them.

❧

1 John 4:16 NLT

As the sun shines on all things on earth in
the same way, yet as if each is separate, that is how
God's love is for each of us: the same yet unique.

St. Thérèse of Lisieux

The life of faith is a daily exploration of
the constant and countless ways in which
God's grace and love are experienced.

Eugene Peterson

Believing that you are loved will set you free
to be who God created you to be.
So rest in His love and just be yourself.

Lisa Whelchel

But God demonstrates His own love toward us,
in that while we were still sinners,
Christ died for us.

Romans 5:8 NKJV

Even before God created the heavens and
the earth, He knew you and me, and He chose us!
You and I were born because
it was God's good pleasure.

Kay Arthur

God does not love us because we are valuable.
We are valuable because God loves us.

Fulton J. Sheen

The fact is, God no longer deals with us in
judgment but in mercy. If people got what they
deserved, this old planet would have ripped apart
at the seams centuries ago. Praise God that
because of His great love "we are not consumed,
for his compassions never fail" (Lam. 3:22).

Joni Eareckson Tada

As the Father loved Me, I also have loved you;
abide in My love.

John 15:9 NKJV

No matter what we've been, when we are touched
by God, we can honestly say,
"Now I'm no longer the same!"

Gloria Gaither

When once we are assured that God is good,
then there can be nothing left to fear.

Hannah Whitall Smith

God loves us the way we are, but
He loves us too much to leave us that way.

Leighton Ford

Our hearts are prone to wander and tempted
to squander our Father's inheritance on
the world's cheap amusements. But, when our eyes
awaken to reality, when we lift our heads above
the compromise, and when our stomachs ache
for the food of home, a certain Father will always
be standing at the gate, ready to prepare
a feast for us, waiting anxiously for
His prodigal to come home.

Beth Moore

But while he was still a long way off,
his father saw him and was filled with
compassion for him; he ran to his son,
threw his arms around him and kissed him.

Luke 15:20 NIV

Grace and God's Word

All Scripture is given
by inspiration of God, and
is profitable for doctrine,
for reproof, for correction,
for instruction in righteousness.

2 Timothy 3:16 KJV

God's Word is unlike any other book. The Bible is a roadmap for life here on earth and for life eternal. As Christians, we are called upon to study God's Holy Word, to trust its promises, to follow its commandments, and to share its Good News with the world.

As women who seek to follow in the footsteps of the One from Galilee, we must study the Bible and meditate upon its meaning for our lives. Otherwise, we deprive ourselves of a priceless gift from our Creator. God's Holy Word is, indeed, a transforming, life-changing, one-of-a-kind treasure. And, a passing acquaintance with the Good Book is insufficient for Christians who seek to obey God's Word and to understand His will.

God's Word is a light not only
to our path but also to our thinking.
Place it in your heart today,
and you will never walk
in darkness.

Joni Eareckson Tada

Every word of God is pure; He is a shield to those
who put their trust in Him.

Proverbs 30:5 NKJV

Walking in faith brings you to the Word of God.
There you will be healed, cleansed, fed,
nurtured, equipped, and matured.

Kay Arthur

There is no way to draw closer to God unless you
are in the Word of God every day. It's your compass.
Your guide. You can't get where
you need to go without it.

Stormie Omartian

For the word of God is living and active.
Sharper than any double-edged sword, it penetrates
even to dividing soul and spirit, joints and marrow;
it judges the thoughts and attitudes of the heart.

Hebrews 4:12 NIV

Voltaire expected that within fifty years of his lifetime there would not be one Bible in the world. Today, his house is a distribution center for Bibles in many languages.

Corrie ten Boom

Unless we form the habit of going to the Bible in bright moments as well as in trouble, we cannot fully respond to its consolations because we lack equilibrium between light and darkness.

Helen Keller

The Scriptures were not given to increase our knowledge but to change our lives.

D. L. Moody

Jesus answered, "It is written: 'Man does not live by bread alone, but on every word that comes from the mouth of God.'"

Matthew 4:4 NIV

The balance of affirmation and
discipline, freedom and restraint,
encouragement and warning
is different for each child
and season and generation, yet
the absolutes of God's Word
are necessary and trustworthy
no matter how mercuric the time.

Gloria Gaither

When we let God's Word seep into
our own lives little by little, it nourishes us
and becomes part of us.

Janette Oke

If you'll flip from cover to cover, you'll notice
that it's overwhelmingly a book of stories—
tales of men and women who walked with God.

John Eldredge

It is less important to ask a Christian what he or
she believes about the Bible
than to inquire what he or she does with it.

Lesslie Newbigin

But prove yourselves doers of the word,
and not merely hearers.

James 1:22 NASB

The Bible is like no other book. Treat it that way!

Marie T. Freeman

The Reference Point for the Christian is the Bible.
All values, judgments, and attitudes must be
gauged in relationship to this Reference Point.

Ruth Bell Graham

The words of the LORD are pure words,
like silver tried in a furnace . . . .

Psalm 12:6 NKJV

Your word is a lamp to my feet
and a light to my path.

Psalm 119:105 NKJV

*A*s we spend time reading,
applying, and obeying our Bibles,
the Spirit of Truth Who
is also the Spirit of Jesus increasingly
reveals Jesus to us.

Anne Graham Lotz

Ask God to help you tune your life every day to
His Word so you can bring harmony
and joy to those around you.

Billy Graham

Don't worry about what you do not understand
of the Bible. Worry about what you
do understand and do not live by.

Corrie ten Boom

Decisions which are made in the light of
God's Word are stable and show wisdom.

Vonette Z. Bright

The Bible is a weapon. It can be used for offense
and defense. When you meet Satan with authority,
the authority of the Word, he will depart.

Corrie ten Boom

Grace and God's Presence

Where can I go from your Spirit?
Where can I flee from your presence?
If I go up to the heavens, you are there;
if I make my bed in the depths,
you are there. If I rise on the wings of
the dawn, if I settle on the far side of
the sea, even there your hand will guide
me, your right hand will hold me fast.

Psalm 139:7-10 NIV

*S*ince God is everywhere, we are free to sense His presence whenever we take the time to quiet our souls and turn our prayers to Him. But sometimes, amid the incessant demands of everyday life, we turn our thoughts far from God; when we do, we suffer.

Do you set aside quiet moments each day to offer praise to your Creator? As a woman who has received the gift of God's grace, you most certainly should. Silence is a gift that you give to yourself *and* to God. During these moments of stillness, you will often sense the infinite love and power of your Creator—and He, in turn, will speak directly to your heart.

The familiar words of Psalm 46:10 remind us to "Be still, and know that I am God." When we do so, we encounter the awesome presence of our loving Heavenly Father, and we are comforted in the knowledge that God is not just near. He is here.

I have acted like I'm all alone,
but the truth is that I never will be.
When my prayers are weak,
God is listening.
When my words are rote,
God is listening.
When my heart is dry,
amazingly God is still listening.

Angela Thomas

As I wander from village to village,
I feel it is no idle fancy that the Master
walks beside me, and I hear his voice saying gently,
"I am with you always, even unto the end."

    Lottie Moon (missionary to China)

Through the death and broken body of Jesus Christ
on the Cross, you and I have been given access
to the presence of God when we approach
Him by faith in prayer.

    Anne Graham Lotz

Pour out your heart to God and tell Him how you
feel. Be real, be honest, and when you get it all out,
you'll start to feel the gradual covering
of God's comforting presence.

    Bill Hybels

Draw near to God, and He will draw near to you.

    James 4:8 HCSB

It is God to whom and with whom we travel,
and while He is the End of our journey,
He is also at every stopping place.

Elisabeth Elliot

I have come to recognize that He never asks us
to do anything He has not already done.
He never takes us anyplace where He has not been
ahead of us. What He is after is not performance
but a relationship with us.

Gloria Gaither

Do not be afraid or discouraged.
For the LORD your God is with you
wherever you go.

Joshua 1:9 NLT

For the eyes of the LORD
range throughout the earth
to strengthen those whose hearts
are fully committed to him.

2 Chronicles 16:9 NIV

Grace comes from the heart of a gracious God
who wants to stun you and overwhelm you with
a gift you don't deserve—salvation, adoption,
a spiritual ability to use in kingdom service,
answered prayer, the church, His presence,
His wisdom, His guidance, His love.

Bill Hybels

A sense of gratitude for God's presence in our lives
will help open our eyes to what he has done in
the past and what he will do in the future.

Emilie Barnes

Until we grieve we cannot be comforted.
Until we lay our longings at the feet of Jesus,
we cannot be ministered to by His presence.

Nicole Johnson

We all go through pain and sorrow,
but the presence of God, like a warm,
comforting blanket, can shield us and protect us,
and allow the deep inner joy to surface,
even in the most devastating circumstances.

Barbara Johnson

Only a love that has no regard for vessels and jars—
appearances or image—only a love that will lavish
its most treasured essence on the feet of Jesus
can produce the kind of fragrance that draws
cynics and believers alike into His presence.

Gloria Gaither

Let your gentleness be evident to all.
The Lord is near.

Philippians 4:5 NIV

Grace and God's Provision

And God will generously provide
all you need. Then you will
always have everything you need
and plenty left over
to share with others.

2 Corinthians 9:8 NLT

As a busy woman, you know from firsthand experience that life is not always easy. But as a recipient of God's grace, you also know that you are protected by a loving Heavenly Father.

In times of trouble, God will comfort you; in times of sorrow, He will dry your tears. When you are troubled or weak or sorrowful, God is neither distant nor disinterested. To the contrary, God is always present and always vitally engaged in the events of your life. Reach out to Him, and build your future on the rock that cannot be shaken . . . trust in God and rely upon His provisions. He can provide everything you really need . . . and far, far more.

*O*ur heavenly Father
wants nothing but the best
for any of us, and only He knows
what that is, for He is All-wise,
the Omniscient.

❧

Elisabeth Elliot

When you live a surrendered life,
God is willing and able to provide
for your every need.

🕮 *Corrie ten Boom*

Steep your life in God-reality, God-initiative,
God-provisions. Don't worry about missing out.
You'll find all your everyday
human concerns will be met.

🕮 *Matthew 6:33* MSG

For the LORD your God has arrived to live
among you. He is a mighty savior.
He will rejoice over you with great gladness.
With his love, he will calm all your fears.
He will exult over you by singing a happy song.

🕮 *Zephaniah 3:17* NLT

Why is love of gold more potent than love of souls?

Lottie Moon (missionary to China)

As faithful stewards of what we have,
ought we not to give earnest thought
to our staggering surplus?

Elisabeth Elliot

Theirs is an endless road, a hopeless maze,
who seek for goods before they seek for God.

St. Bernard of Clairvaux

I have shown you in every way, by laboring like
this, that you must support the weak.
And remember the words of the Lord Jesus,
that He said, "It is more blessed to give
than to receive."

Acts 20:35 NKJV

We are made spiritually lethargic
by a steady diet of materialism.

Mary Morrison Suggs

It's sobering to contemplate how much time, effort, sacrifice, compromise, and attention we give to acquiring and increasing our supply of something that is totally insignificant in eternity.

Anne Graham Lotz

When we put people before possessions in our hearts, we are sowing seeds of enduring satisfaction.

Beverly LaHaye

Which of you by taking thought can add one cubit unto his stature? And why take ye thought for raiment? Consider the lilies of the field, how they grow; they toil not, neither do they spin: and yet I say unto you, That even Solomon in all his glory was not arrayed like one of these. Wherefore, if God so clothe the grass of the field, which today is, and tomorrow is cast into the oven, shall he not much more clothe you, O ye of little faith?

Matthew 6:27-30 KJV

I have held many things in my hands,
and I have lost them all; but whatever I have placed
in God's hands, that I still possess.

        Corrie ten Boom

He is no fool who gives what he cannot keep
to gain what he cannot lose.

        Jim Elliot

Our ultimate aim in life is not to be healthy,
wealthy, prosperous, or problem free.
Our ultimate aim in life is to bring glory to God.

        Anne Graham Lotz

No one can serve two masters. The person will
hate one master and love the other, or will follow
one master and refuse to follow the other.
You cannot serve both God and worldly riches.

        Matthew 6:24 NCV

Grace and God's Timing

To every thing there is a season,
and a time to every purpose under
the heaven: . . . A time to weep,
and a time to laugh; a time to mourn,
and a time to dance; . . . A time to love,
and a time to hate; a time of war,
and a time of peace.

Ecclesiastes 3:1, 4, 8 KJV

*I*f you sincerely seek to be a woman of faith, then you must trust God's timing. You will be sorely tempted, however, to do otherwise. Because you are a fallible human being, you are impatient for things to happen. But, God knows better.

God has created a world that unfolds according to His own timetable not ours . . . thank goodness! We mortals might make a terrible mess of things. God does not.

God's plan does not always happen in the way that we would like or at the time of our own choosing. Our task—as believing Christians who trust in a benevolent, all-knowing Father—is to wait patiently for God to reveal Himself. And reveal Himself He will. Always. But until God's perfect plan is made known, we must walk in faith and never lose hope. And we must continue to trust Him. Always.

God manages perfectly,
day and night, year in and year out,
the movements of the stars,
the wheeling of the planets,
the staggering coordination
of events that goes on at
the molecular level in order to hold
things together. There is no doubt
that He can manage the timing
of my days and weeks.

Elisabeth Elliot

Waiting is an essential part of spiritual discipline.
It can be the ultimate test of faith.

Anne Graham Lotz

God knows not only what we need but also
when we need it. His timing is always perfect.

Elisabeth Elliot

Events of all sorts creep or fly exactly
as God pleases.

William Cowper

Humble yourselves, therefore,
under God's mighty hand,
that he may lift you up in due time.

1 Peter 5:6 NIV

Life's unfolding stops for no one.

Kathy Troccoli

Our time is short! The time we can invest for God,
in creative things, in receiving our fellowmen
for Christ, is short!

Billy Graham

God has a present will for your life. It is neither
chaotic nor utterly exhausting. In the midst of
many good choices vying for your time,
He will give you the discernment
to recognize what is best.

Beth Moore

Our leisure, even our play, is a matter of
serious concern. There is no neutral ground in
the universe: every square inch, every split second,
is claimed by God and counterclaimed by Satan.

C. S. Lewis

When we read of the great Biblical leaders,
we see that it was not uncommon for God to
ask them to wait, not just a day or two but
for years, until God was ready for them to act.

☙ *Gloria Gaither*

We must leave it to God to answer our prayers
in His own wisest way. Sometimes, we are so
impatient and think that God does not answer.
God always answers! He never fails!
Be still. Abide in Him.

☙ *Mrs. Charles E. Cowman*

God does not hasten His works.
He does all things in their time.

☙ *St. Vincent de Paul*

Wait patiently on the LORD.
Be brave and courageous.
Yes, wait patiently on the LORD.

☙ *Psalm 27:14 NLT*

We must learn to move
according to the timetable
of the Timeless One,
and to be at peace.

Elisabeth Elliot

Make each day useful and cheerful and prove that
you know the worth of time by employing it well.
Then youth will be happy, old age without regret,
and life a beautiful success.

✿ *Louisa May Alcott*

Waiting is an essential part of spiritual discipline.
It can be the ultimate test of faith.

✿ *Anne Graham Lotz*

This is what the LORD says:
"In the time of my favor I will answer you,
and in the day of salvation I will help you."

✿ *Isaiah 49:8 NIV*

Grace and God's Mercy

But because of his great love
for us, God, who is rich in mercy,
made us alive with Christ even when
we were dead in transgressions—
it is by grace you have been saved.

Ephesians 2:4-5 NIV

God's ability to forgive is as infinite as His love. Romans 3:23 reminds us of a universal truth: "All have sinned, and come short of the glory of God" (KJV). All of us, even the most righteous among us, are sinners. But despite our imperfections, our Father in heaven offers us salvation through the person of His Son.

God sent Jesus to die so that we might have eternal life. As Christians, we have been blessed by a merciful, loving God. May we accept His mercy. And may we, in turn, show love and mercy to our friends, to our families, and to all whom He chooses to place in our paths.

For God is, indeed,
a wonderful Father who longs
to pour out His mercy upon us,
and whose majesty is so great
that He can transform us
from deep within.

St. Teresa of Avila

God "longs to be gracious" to us (Isaiah 30:18),
and He carries out His judgment against our sin
with holy sorrow, intending His discipline
to be a vehicle of mercy toward us.

Nancy Groom

Mercy is not the ability to no longer feel the pain
and heartache of living in this world.
Mercy is knowing that I am being held
through the pain by my Father.

Angela Thomas

So let us come boldly to the throne of
our gracious God. There we will receive his mercy,
and we will find grace to help us when we need it.

Hebrews 4:16 NLT

The eternal plan to reconcile man with God and
bridge the separation, to save him from judgment
for that sin, to forgive him of all sins,
originated in the heart of God.

Anne Graham Lotz

There is nothing that God cannot forgive except
for the rejection of Christ. No matter how black
the sin, how hideous the sin, if we but confess it to
Him in true repentance and faith, He will forgive.
He will accept and forgive.

Ruth Bell Graham

Man lives by getting and forgetting.
God lives by giving and forgiving.

Diana Baskin

How happy we are when we realize that
He is responsible, that He goes before,
that goodness and mercy shall follow us!

Mrs. Charles E. Cowman

No trail is too great, no temptation is too strong,
but that Jesus Christ can give us the mercy
and the grace that we need, when we need it.

Warren Wiersbe

When terrible things happen, there are
two choices, and only two: We can trust God,
or we can defy Him. We believe that God is God,
He's still got the whole world in His hands
and knows exactly what He's doing, or we must
believe that He is not God and that
we are at the awful mercy of mere chance.

Elisabeth Elliot

And the LORD said,
"I will cause all my goodness to pass
in front of you, and I will proclaim
my name, the LORD, in your presence.
I will have mercy on whom I will have
mercy, and I will have compassion
on whom I will have compassion."

Exodus 33:19 NIV

In heaven, we will see that nothing,
absolutely nothing, was wasted,
and that every tear counted
and every cry was heard.

Joni Eareckson Tada

Grace and Jesus

Therefore if any man be in Christ,
he is a new creature:
old things are passed away;
behold, all things are become new.

2 Corinthians 5:17 KJV

The 19th-century writer Hannah Whitall Smith observed, "The crucial question for each of us is this: What do you think of Jesus, and do you yet have a personal acquaintance with Him?" Indeed, the answer to that question determines the quality, the course, and the direction of our lives today and for all eternity.

The old familiar hymn begins, "What a friend we have in Jesus." No truer words were ever penned. Jesus is the sovereign Friend and ultimate savior of mankind. Christ showed enduring love for His believers by willingly sacrificing His own life so that we might have eternal life. Now, it is *our* turn to become *His* friend.

Let us love our Savior, praise Him, and share His message of salvation with our neighbors and with the world. When we do, we demonstrate that our acquaintance with the Master is not a passing fancy; it is, instead, the cornerstone and the touchstone of our lives.

I will sing the wondrous story
Of the Christ who died for me;
How He left His home in glory
For the cross of Calvary.

Francis H. Rowley

Here is our opportunity: we cannot see God,
but we can see Christ. Christ was not only
the Son of God, but He was the Father.
Whatever Christ was, that God is.

Hannah Whitall Smith

Our neat and tidy God-in-a-box ideas about Jesus
must be put aside as we seek after the real Christ,
the one who won't fit in a tomb, who is both
small enough to climb into our hearts
and big enough to save the entire world.

Liz Curtis Higgs

Rejoice, that the immortal God is born,
so that mortal man may live in eternity.

Jan Hus

Christ has made my soul beautiful with
the jewels of grace and virtue.
I belong to Him whom the angels serve.

St. Agnes

Jesus loves me! This I know, for the Bible
tells me so. Little ones to him belong;
they are weak, but he is strong. Yes, Jesus loves me!
Yes, Jesus loves me! Yes, Jesus loves me!
The Bible tells me so.

Anna B. Warner and Susan Warner

Jesus makes God visible. But that truth does not
make Him somehow less than God.
He is equally supreme with God.

Anne Graham Lotz

In the beginning was the Word,
and the Word was with God,
and the Word was God . . . .
And the Word was made flesh,
and dwelt among us,
(and we beheld his glory,
the glory as of the only
begotten of the Father,)
full of grace and truth.

John 1:1,14 KJV

We have heard the joyful sound,
spread the tidings all around: Jesus saves!

Priscilla J. Owens

I am truly happy with Jesus Christ.
I couldn't live without Him.
When my life gets beyond the ability to cope,
He takes over.

Ruth Bell Graham

There was One, who for "us sinners and
our salvation," left the glories of heaven and
sojourned upon this earth in weariness and woe,
amid those who hated him and finally took his life.

Lottie Moon

Jesus: the proof of God's love.

Philip Yancey

Christians see sin for what it is: willful rebellion
against the rulership of God in their lives.
And in turning from their sin, they have embraced
God's only means of dealing with sin: Jesus.

Kay Arthur

O come, all ye faithful, joyful and triumphant;
O come, let us adore Him, Christ the Lord!

John Francis Wade

God lifted him high and honored him far beyond
anyone or anything, ever, so that all created beings
in heaven and earth, even those long ago dead and
buried, will bow in worship before this Jesus Christ,
and call out in praise that he is the Master of all,
to the glorious honor of God the Father.

Philippians 2:9-11 MSG

In your greatest weakness,
turn to your greatest strength,
Jesus, and hear Him say,
"My grace is sufficient for you,
for My strength is made perfect in
weakness"(2 Corinthians 12:9 NKJV).

Lisa Whelchel

When we are in a situation where Jesus
is all we have, we soon discover
He is all we really need.

✿ *Gigi Graham Tchividjian*

Jesus Christ is the same yesterday, today,
and forever.

✿ *Hebrews 13:8* HCSB

To God be the glory, great things He has done;
So loved He the world that He gave us His Son.

✿ *Fanny Crosby*

In this world you will have trouble.
But take heart! I have overcome the world.

✿ *John 16:33* NIV

Christ is the horn of our salvation, the One who was secured on a cross so that we could be secured in the Lamb's book of Life.

Beth Moore

I have been all over the world, and I have never met anyone who regretted giving his or her life to Christ.

Billy Graham

Just as I am, without one plea, but that Thy blood was shed for me.
And that Thou bid'st me come to Thee, O Lamb of God, I come! I come!

Charlotte Elliott

I am the Vine,
you are the branches.
When you're joined with me
and I with you, the relation intimate
and organic, the harvest
is sure to be abundant.

John 15:5 MSG

Grace and God's People

For where two or three come together
in my name, there am I with them.

Matthew 18:20 NIV

Fellowship with other believers should be an integral part of your everyday life. Your association with fellow Christians should be uplifting, enlightening, encouraging, and consistent.

Are you an active member of your fellowship? Are you a builder of bridges inside the four walls of your church *and* outside it? Do you contribute to God's glory by contributing your time and your talents to a close-knit band of believers? Hopefully so. The fellowship of believers is intended to be a powerful tool for spreading God's Good News and uplifting His children. And God intends for you to be a fully contributing member of that fellowship. Your intentions should be the same.

Every time a new person comes
to God, every time someone's
gifts find expression in the fellowship
of believers, every time a family
in need is surrounded by the caring
church, the truth is affirmed anew:
the Church triumphant
is alive and well!

Gloria Gaither

Be filled with the Holy Spirit; join a church where the members believe the Bible and know the Lord; seek the fellowship of other Christians; learn and be nourished by God's Word and His many promises. Conversion is not the end of your journey—it is only the beginning.

Corrie ten Boom

It is a true sign of the church when true Christians love one another. The church is to be a loving church in a dying culture.

Francis Schaeffer

Our churches are meant to be havens where the caste rules of the world do not apply.

Beth Moore

The house of God is not a safe place. It is a cross where time and eternity meet, and where we are— or should be—challenged to live more vulnerably, more interdependently.

Madeleine L'Engle

Only participation in the full life of a local church builds spiritual muscle.

Rick Warren

One of the ways God refills us after failure is through the blessing of Christian fellowship. Just experiencing the joy of simple activities shared with other children of God can have a healing effect on us.

Anne Graham Lotz

Be united with other Christians.
A wall with loose bricks
is not good. The bricks must be
cemented together.

Corrie ten Boom

Now you are Christ's body,
and individually members of it.

1 Corinthians 12:27 NASB

Today, some of the hardest groups of people
to reach are not the Jews but those who have gone
to church all their lives, are familiar with
the Gospel story, converse using spiritual clichés,
and sing the traditional hymns of faith from
memory, yet have never truly placed
their faith in Jesus Christ.

Anne Graham Lotz

I'm not sure anything outweighs the importance of
authenticity in the home, particularly to
young people who are raised in a churchgoing or
Christian home.

Beth Moore

*G*od wants to be in
our leisure time as much as
He is in our churches
and in our work.

Beth Moore

Be on guard for yourselves and for all the flock,
among which the Holy Spirit has made you
overseers, to shepherd the church of God
which He purchased with His own blood.

Acts 20:28 NASB

Theology is an interesting school of thought.
The Bible is beautiful literature. Sitting in a quiet
sanctuary, bathed in the amber light from
stained-glass windows, having our jangled nerves
soothed by the chords from an organ—all that is
inspiring. But, to tell you the truth, when we leave
the classroom, close the church door, and walk out
into the real world, it is the indisputable proof
of changed lives that makes us believers.

Gloria Gaither

It is not the business of the church to adapt
Christ to men but men to Christ.

Dorothy Sayers

For we are God's fellow workers;
you are God's field,
you are God's building.

1 Corinthians 3:9 NKJV

Grace and God's Strength

The LORD is the strength of my life.

Psalm 27:1 KJV

Have you made God the cornerstone of your life, or is He relegated to a few hours on Sunday morning? Have you genuinely allowed God to reign over every corner of your heart, or have you attempted to place Him in a spiritual compartment? The answer to these questions will determine the direction of your day and your life.

God loves you. In times of trouble, He will comfort you; in times of sorrow, He will dry your tears. When you are weak or sorrowful, God is as near as your next breath. He stands at the door of your heart and waits. Welcome Him in and allow Him to rule. And then, accept the peace and the strength and the protection and the abundance that only God can give.

*Y*ou are mighty, Lord,
you are mighty.
Nothing compares to you
in power. No one can equal
the strength of your hand.

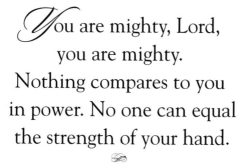

Mary Morrison Suggs

God walks with us. He scoops us up in His arms
or simply sits with us in silent strength
until we cannot avoid the awesome recognition
that yes, even now, He is here.

Gloria Gaither

No giant will ever be a match for a big God
with a little rock.

Beth Moore

Have you not known? Have you not heard?
The everlasting God, the Lord, the Creator of
the ends of the earth, neither faints nor is weary.
His understanding is unsearchable. He gives power
to the weak, and to those who have no might
He increases strength. Even the youths shall faint
and be weary, and the young men shall utterly fall,
but those who wait on the Lord shall renew
their strength; they shall mount up with wings
like eagles, they shall run and not be weary,
they shall walk and not faint.

Isaiah 40:28-31 NKJV

The last and greatest lesson that the soul has to
learn is the fact that God, and God alone,
is enough for all its needs. This is the lesson
that all His dealings with us are meant to teach;
and this is the crowning discovery of our whole
Christian life. God is enough!

Hannah Whitall Smith

Your strength, my weakness—here they always
meet, When I lay down my burden at Your feet:
The things that seem to crush will in the end
Be seen as rungs on which I did ascend!
Thank You, Lord.

Corrie ten Boom

For the LORD your God is God of gods
and Lord of lords, the great God,
mighty and awesome.

Deuteronomy 10:17 NIV

All the power of God—
the same power that hung
the stars in place and put the planets
in their courses and transformed
Earth—now resides in you to energize
and strengthen you to become
the person God created you to be.

Anne Graham Lotz

If you believe in a God who controls the big things,
you have to believe in a God who controls
the little things. It is we, of course,
to whom things look "little" or "big."

Elisabeth Elliot

God is able, especially when you are not.

Susan Wales

We have a God who delights in impossibilities.

Andrew Murray

Jesus looked at them and said,
"With man this is impossible,
but with God all things are possible."

Matthew 19:26 NIV

When Jesus is in our midst, He brings His limitless
power along as well. But, Jesus must be in
the middle, all eyes and hearts focused on Him.

Shirley Dobson

The power of God through His Spirit will work
within us to the degree that we permit it.

Mrs. Charles E. Cowman

He upholds the whole creation, founded
the earth, and still sustains it by the word of His
power. What cannot He do in the affairs of families
and kingdoms, far beyond our conception and
expectation, who hangs the earth upon nothing?

Matthew Henry

I pray also that you will have greater understanding
in your heart so you will know the hope to which
he has called us and that you will know how rich
and glorious are the blessings God has promised
his holy people. And you will know that
God's power is very great for us who believe.

Ephesians 1:18-19 NCV

*Y*ou are the God who does wonders;
You have declared
Your strength among the peoples.

❧

Psalm 77:14 NKJV

"But David encouraged himself in the Lord
his God": and the result was a magnificent victory
in which all that they had lost was more than
restored to them. This always will be and always
must be the result of a courageous faith, because
faith lays hold of the omnipotence of God.

Hannah Whitall Smith

As we join together in prayer, we draw on
God's enabling might in a way that multiplies
our own efforts many times over.

Shirley Dobson

If we take God's program, we can have
God's power—not otherwise.

E. Stanley Jones

The LORD is my strength and my song;
he has become my victory. He is my God,
and I will praise him.

Exodus 15:2 NLT

Grace and God's Promises

Let us hold on to the confession
of our hope without wavering,
for He who promised is faithful.

Hebrews 10:23 HCSB

God's grace is the ultimate gift, and we owe Him our eternal gratitude. Our Heavenly Father is waiting patiently for each of us to accept His Son and receive His grace. Let us accept that gift today so that we might enjoy God's presence now and throughout all eternity.

The Bible contains promises, made by God, upon which we, as believers, can and must depend. But sometimes, especially when we find ourselves caught in the inevitable entanglements of life, we fail to trust God completely.

Are you tired? Discouraged? Fearful? Be comforted and trust the promises that God has made to you. Are you worried or anxious? Be confident in God's power. Do you see a difficult future ahead? Be courageous and call upon God. He will protect you and then use you according to His purposes. Are you confused? Listen to the quiet voice of your Heavenly Father. He is not a God of confusion. Talk with Him; listen to Him; trust Him, and trust His promises. He is steadfast, and He is your Protector . . . forever.

Brother, is your faith
looking upward today?
Trust in the promise of the Savior.
Sister, is the light shining bright
on your way? Trust in the promise
of thy Lord.

Fanny Crosby

Claim all of God's promises in the Bible.
Your sins, your worries, your life—
you may cast them all on Him.

         Corrie ten Boom

We have ample evidence that the Lord is able
to guide. The promises cover every imaginable
situation. All we need to do is to take
the hand he stretches out.

         Elisabeth Elliot

As for God, his way is perfect. All the LORD's
promises prove true. He is a shield for all
who look to him for protection.

         Psalm 18:30 NLT

Lord, I thank you for the promise of heaven
and the unexpected moments when you
touch my heartstrings with that longing
for my eternal home.

      Joni Eareckson Tada

Christ still asks for total surrender and
then promises His gift of full, overflowing joy.

      Catherine Marshall

No matter what we are going through,
no matter how long the waiting for answers,
of one thing we may be sure. God is faithful.
He keeps His promises. What He starts,
He finishes . . . including His perfect work in us.

      Gloria Gaither

Shake the dust from your past,
and move forward in His promises.

Kay Arthur

God has promised that if we harvest well
with the tools of thanksgiving, there
will be seeds for planting in the spring.

Gloria Gaither

Thanksgiving or complaining—these words express
two contrastive attitudes of the souls of God's
children in regard to His dealings with them.
The soul that gives thanks can find comfort in
everything; the soul that complains
can find comfort in nothing.

Hannah Whitall Smith

Peace is full confidence that God is
Who He says He is and that He will keep
every promise in His Word.

Dorothy Harrison Pentecost

Come unto me,
all ye that labor
and are heavy laden,
and I will give you rest.

Matthew 11:28 KJV

And Finally . . .

Grace to you and peace from
God our Father
and the Lord Jesus Christ.

Philippians 1:2 NASB

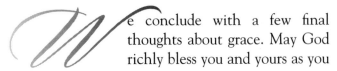

e conclude with a few final thoughts about grace. May God richly bless you and yours as you continue on your journey.

Turn your eyes upon Jesus, and the things
of earth will grow strangely dim in the light
of His glory and grace.

Helen H. Lemmel

Teaching that lacks grace may enter our ears,
but it never reaches the heart. When the grace of
God really touches our inmost mind so as to bring
understanding, then the word that reaches
our ear can also sink deeply into the heart.

Isidore of Seville

The marvelous thing is that this holiness is nothing
we can earn. We don't become holy by acquiring
merit badges and Brownie points. It has nothing
to do with virtue or job description or morality.
It is nothing we can do, in this do-it-yourself world.
It is gift, sheer gift, waiting there to be recognized
and received. We do not have to be
qualified to be holy.

Madeleine L'Engle

We are here to be living monuments to God's grace.

      Oswald Chambers

God "longs to be gracious" to us (Isaiah 30:18),
and He carries out His judgment against our sin
with holy sorrow, intending His discipline
to be a vehicle of mercy toward us.

      Nancy Groom

God does amazing works through prayers
that seek to extend His grace to others.

      Shirley Dobson

*W*hat grace calls you to do,
grace provides.
Grace is power.

✍

Kay Arthur

And the God of all grace, who called you to
his eternal glory in Christ, after you have suffered
a little while, will himself restore you
and make you strong, firm and steadfast.

1 Peter 5:10 NIV

My grace is sufficient for you,
for My strength is made perfect in weakness.

2 Corinthians 12:9 NKJV

Saving is all [God's] idea, and all his work.
All we do is trust him enough to let him do it.
It's God's idea from start to finish! We don't play
the major role. If we did, we'd probably go around
bragging that we'd done the whole thing!
No, we neither make nor save ourselves.
God does both the making and the saving.

Ephesians 2:8-9 MSG

For it is by grace you have
been saved, through faith—
and this not from yourselves,
it is the gift of God—
not by works,
so that no one can boast.

Ephesians 2:8-9 NIV

*M*arvelous, infinite,
matchless grace, freely bestowed
on all who believe!
God's grace that will pardon
and cleanse within!

Julia H. Johnston